HAL•LEONARD
Classical
PLAY-ALONG™

Volume 18

Johann Sebastian
BACH
(1685-1750)

T0061382

Flute Sonata in Eb Major

The Hal Leonard Classical Play-Along™ series allows you to work through great classical works systematically and at any tempo with accompaniment.

Tracks 2-4 on the CD demonstrate the concert version of each movement. After tuning your instrument to Track 1 you can begin practicing the piece. Using the Amazing Slow-Downer technology included on the CD, you can adjust the recording to any tempo you like without altering the pitch. (Note that when using Amazing Slow-Downer, the CD will stop after each track instead of playing continuously.)

- Track No. 1 – tuning notes
- Track numbers in circles ◯ – concert version
- Track numbers in diamonds ◆ – play-along version

CONCERT VERSION

Evelin Degen, Flute

Sigrun Stephan, Harpsichord

ISBN 978-1-4234-8892-7

HAL•LEONARD®
CORPORATION

7777 W. BLUEMOUND RD. P.O. BOX 13819 MILWAUKEE, WI 53213

In Australia Contact:
Hal Leonard Australia Pty. Ltd.
4 Lentara Court
Cheltenham, Victoria, 3192 Australia
Email: ausadmin@halleonard.com.au

Visit Hal Leonard Online at
www.halleonard.com

SONATA

for Flute in Eb Major, BWV 1031

I

J.S. Bach (1685–1750)

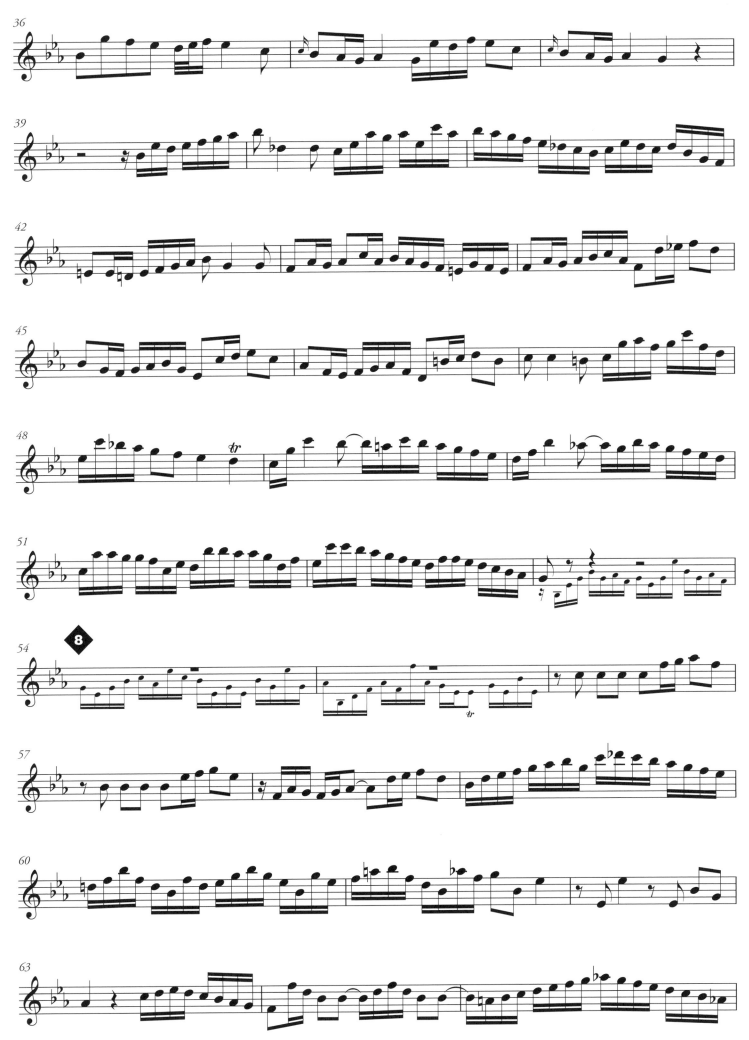

Hal·Leonard Classical PLAY-ALONG™

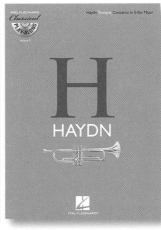

MOZART

HAYDN

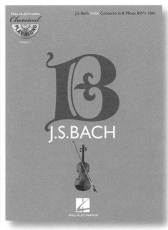

J.S.BACH

VIVALDI

BRAHMS

BEETHOVEN

The Hal Leonard Classical Play-Along™ series will help you play great classical pieces. Listen to the full performance tracks to hear how the piece sounds with an orchestra, and then play along using the accompaniment tracks. The audio CD is playable on any CD player. For PC and Mac computer users, the CD is enhanced so you can adjust the recording to any tempo without changing pitch.

1. MOZART:
FLUTE CONCERTO IN D MAJOR, K314
Book/CD Pack
00842341 Flute......................$12.95

2. SAMMARTINI:
DESCANT (SOPRANO) RECORDER
CONCERTO IN F MAJOR
Book/CD Pack
00842342 Soprano Recorder..................$12.95

3. LOEILLET:
TREBLE (ALTO) RECORDER
SONATA IN G MAJOR, OP.1, NO.3
Book/CD Pack
00842343 Alto Recorder....................$12.95

4. MOZART:
CLARINET CONCERTO IN A MAJOR, K622
Book/CD Pack
00842344 Clarinet....................$12.95

5. HAYDN:
TRUMPET CONCERTO IN B-FLAT MAJOR
Book/CD Pack
00842345 Trumpet....................$12.95

6. MOZART:
HORN CONCERTO IN D MAJOR, K412/514
Book/CD Pack
00842346 Horn....................$12.95

7. BACH:
VIOLIN CONCERTO IN A MINOR, BWV 1041
Book/CD Pack
00842347 Violin....................$12.95

8. TELEMANN:
VIOLA CONCERTO IN G MAJOR, TWV 51:G9
Book/CD Pack
00842348 Viola....................$12.95

9. HAYDN:
CELLO CONCERTO IN C MAJOR, HOB. VIIB: 1
Book/CD Pack
00842349 Cello....................$12.95

10. BACH:
PIANO CONCERTO IN F MINOR, BWV 1056
Book/CD Pack
00842350 Piano....................$12.95

11. PERGOLESI:
FLUTE CONCERTO IN G MAJOR
Book/CD Pack
00842351 Flute....................$12.95

12. BARRE:
DESCANT (SOPRANO) RECORDER
SUITE NO. 9 "DEUXIEME LIVRE" G MAJOR
Book/CD Pack
00842352 Soprano Recorder..................$12.95

13. VIVALDI:
TREBLE (ALTO) RECORDER CONCERTO
IN A MINOR RV 108
Book/CD Pack
00842353 Alto Recorder....................$12.95

14. VON WEBER:
CLARINET CONCERTO NO. 1 IN F MINOR, OP. 73
Book/CD Pack
00842354 Clarinet....................$12.95

15. MOZART:
VIOLIN CONCERTO IN G MAJOR, K216
Book/CD Pack
00842355 Violin....................$12.95

16. BOCCHERINI:
CELLO CONCERTO IN B-FLAT MAJOR, G482
Book/CD Pack
00842356 Cello....................$12.95

17. MOZART:
PIANO CONCERTO IN C MAJOR, K467
Book/CD Pack
00842357 Piano....................$12.95

18. BACH:
FLUTE SONATA IN E-FLAT MAJOR, BWV 1031
Book/CD Pack
00842450 Flute....................$12.99

19. BRAHMS:
CLARINET SONATA IN F MINOR, OP. 120, NO. 1
Book/CD Pack
00842451 Clarinet....................$12.99

20. BEETHOVEN:
TWO ROMANCES FOR VIOLIN,
OP. 40 IN G & OP. 50 IN F
Book/CD Pack
00842452 Violin....................$12.99

21. MOZART:
PIANO CONCERTO IN D MINOR, K466
Book/CD Pack
00842453 Piano....................$12.99

FOR MORE INFORMATION,
SEE YOUR LOCAL MUSIC DEALER,
OR WRITE TO:

HAL·LEONARD®
CORPORATION
7777 W. BLUEMOUND RD. P.O. BOX 13819
MILWAUKEE, WISCONSIN 53213

Prices, content, and availability subject to change without notice.

www.halleonard.com

World's Great Classical Music

This ambitious series is comprised entirely of new editions of some of the world's most beloved classical music. Each volume includes dozens of selections by the major talents in the history of European art music: Bach, Beethoven, Berlioz, Brahms, Debussy, Dvořák, Handel, Haydn, Mahler, Mendelssohn, Mozart, Rachmaninoff, Schubert, Schumann, Tchaikovsky, Verdi, Vivaldi, and dozens of other composers.

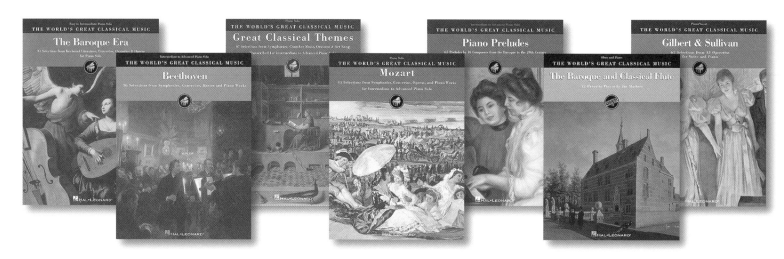

Easy to Intermediate Piano

The Baroque Era
00240057 Piano Solo $14.95

Beethoven
00220034 Piano Solo $14.95

The Classical Era
00240061 Piano Solo $14.95

Classical Masterpieces
00290520 Piano Solo $14.95

Easier Piano Classics
00290519 Piano Solo $16.99

Favorite Classical Themes
00220021 Piano Solo $15.95

Great Easier Piano Literature
00310304 Piano Solo $15.99

Mozart – Simplified Piano Solos
00220028 Piano Solo $14.95

Opera's Greatest Melodies
00220023 Piano Solo $14.95

The Romantic Era
00240068 Piano Solo $14.95

Johann Strauss
00220040 Piano Solo $14.95

The Symphony
00220041 Piano Solo $14.95

Tchaikovsky – Simplified Piano Solos
00220027 Piano Solo $14.95

Intermediate to Advanced Piano

Bach
00220037 Piano Solo $14.95

The Baroque Era
00240060 Piano Solo $14.95

Beethoven
00220033 Piano Solo $15.95

The Classical Era
00240063 Piano Solo $14.95

Great Classical Themes
00310300 Piano Solo $14.95

Great Masterworks
00220020 Piano Solo $14.95

Great Piano Literature
00310302 Piano Solo $14.95

Mozart
00220025 Piano Solo $14.95

Opera at the Piano
00310297 Piano Solo $16.95

Piano Classics
00290518 Piano Solo $14.95

Piano Preludes
00240248 Piano Solo $16.95

The Romantic Era
00240096 Piano Solo $14.95

Johann Strauss
00220035 Piano Solo $14.95

The Symphony
00220032 Piano Solo $14.95

Tchaikovsky
00220026 Piano Solo $14.95

Instrumental

The Baroque and Classical Flute
00841550 Flute and Piano..................$16.95

Masterworks for Guitar
00699503 Classical Guitar $16.95

The Romantic Flute
00240210 Flute and Piano..................$14.99

Vocal

Gilbert & Sullivan
00740142 Piano/Vocal........................$19.99

Prices, content, and availability subject to change without notice.

FOR MORE INFORMATION, SEE YOUR LOCAL MUSIC DEALER, OR WRITE TO:

HAL•LEONARD®
CORPORATION
7777 W. BLUEMOUND RD. P.O. BOX 13819
MILWAUKEE, WISCONSIN 53213

www.halleonard.com